Elizabeth M. Potter / Beatrix Potter

Beatrix Potter Painting Book part 1

AF176077

by
Elizabeth M. Potter

Content   Page

Colouring pictures

I.	The Tale of Benjamin Bunny	3
II.	The Tale of the Flopsy Bunnies	11
III.	The Tale of Peter Rabbit	19
IV.	The Tale of Mr. Jeremy Fisher	27
V.	Original book illustrations	35
VI.	Further books of Elizabeth M. Potter	40

Bibliografische Information der Deutschen Nationalbibliothek:
Die Deutsche Nationalbibliothek verzeichnet diese Publikation in der Deutschen Nationalbibliografie; detaillierte bibliografische Daten sind im Internet über http://dnb.dnb.de abrufbar.

© 2018 Elizabeth M. Potter 1. Auflage
Covergrafik, Texte und Bilder: © 2018 Elizabeth M. Potter

Herstellung und Verlag: BoD – Books on Demand, Norderstedt

ISBN: 9783752866315